To the loving memory of Snowball I:
We hope you get free cable
in kitty heaven.

SIMPSONS COMICS ON PARADE Copyright ©1996 & 1998 by
Bongo Entertainment, Inc. All rights reserved.
No part of this book may be used or reproduced in any manner whatsoever
without written permission except in the case of brief quotations
embodied in critical articles and reviews. For information address:
Bongo Comics Group c/o Titan Books
1999 Avenue of the Stars, Los Angeles, CA 90067

Published in the UK by Titan Books Ltd., 42-44 Dolben Street,
London SE1 0UP, under licence from Bongo Entertainment, Inc.

FIRST EDITION: JUNE 1998

ISBN 1-85286-955-0
8 10 9 7

Publisher: MATT GROENING
Managing Editor: JASON GRODE
Art Director / Editor: BILL MORRISON
Book Design: MARILYN FRANDSEN
Legal Guardian: SUSAN GRODE

Contributing Artists:
PETER ALEXANDER, TIM BAVINGTON, JEANNINE CROWELL BLACK,
SHAUN CASHMAN, STEPHANIE GLADDEN, CARL HARMON, TIM HARKINS,
NATHAN KANE, BILL MORRISON, PHIL ORTIZ, CHRIS UNGAR

Contributing Writers:
JAMIE ANGELL, JACKIE BEHAN, TERRY DELEGEANE, JEFF FILGO,
SCOTT M. GIMPLE, TODD J. GREENWALD, ROB HAMMERSLEY, TIM MAILE,
BILL MORRISON, CHRIS SIMMONS, MARY TRAINOR, DOUG TUBER

PRINTED IN ITALY

CONTENTS

SIMPSONS #24

- **8** SEND IN THE CLOWNS
- **32** HOMEY ALONE
- **37** THE UNBEARABLE LIGHTNESS OF BARNEY

SIMPSONS #25

- **40** MARGE ATTACKS!
- **61** DINER VIOLATIONS
- **64** GAME CALLED BECAUSE OF PAIN

SIMPSONS #26

- **70** GET OFF THE BUS!
- **91** TALES OF THE BRINY DEEP

SIMPSONS #27

- **98** THEY FIXED HOMER'S BRAIN!

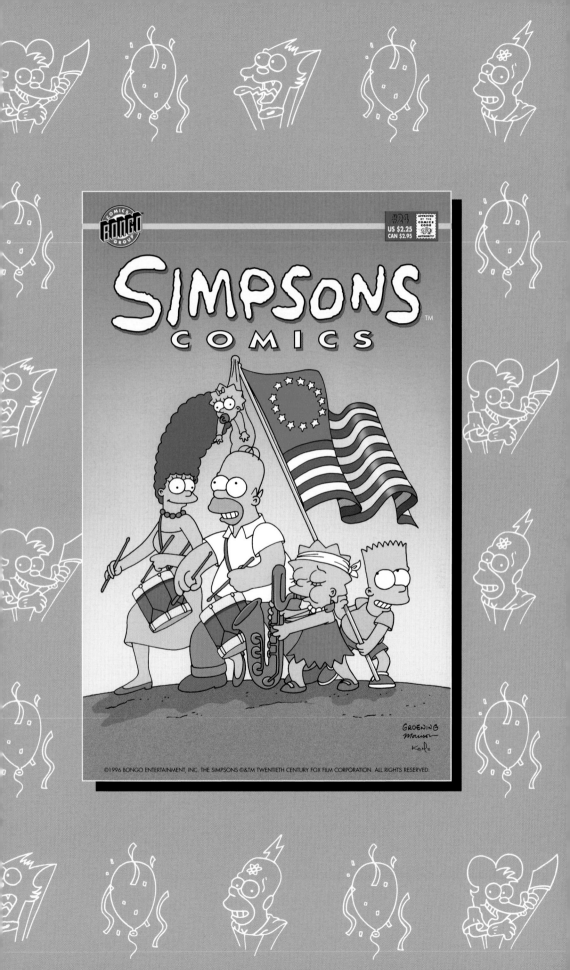

MOM! HOMER! **COME QUICK!!!**

LOOK WHAT'S ON TV!

HURRY, NED! THEY'VE INTERRUPTED THE *JUDGMENTAL HOUR* FOR A NEWS ALERT!

WE INTERRUPT OUR NORMALLY SCHEDULED PROGRAMMING TO BRING YOU THIS SPECIAL BULLETIN.

Don't panic yet, this is just a

SPECIAL BULLETIN!

LOCAL RESIDENTS OF SPRINGFIELD ARE WARNED THERE IS A POTENTIALLY DEVASTATING MASS OF *HOT AIR* APPROACHING FROM THE SOUTHEAST...

...CITIZENS ARE ASKED TO REMAIN IN THEIR HOMES AND TO TAKE THE NECESSARY PRECAUTIONS TO AVOID DIRECT EXPOSURE TO THIS *NOXIOUS, GASEOUS FILIBUSTER*.

...BE EXTRA CAREFUL TO KEEP PETS, SMALL CHILDREN AND BIG BABIES INDOORS. AND IF KNOW ANY ELDERLY PEOPLE...

...TRY TO WARN THEM--EVEN THOU YOU KNOW THEY WON'T LISTEN YOU. THIS IS KENT BROCKMAN WISHING YOU GOOD LUCK AND GOODBYE.

OH, MY GOSH! IT'S *"CAMPAIGN USA"*!!! THE PRESIDENTIAL CANDIDATES THEMSELVES HAVE COME TO SPRINGFIELD TO VIE FOR THE *HIGHEST OFFICE* OF OUR GREAT NATION! WHY, WE'LL GET A FIRST-HAND LOOK AT *DEMOCRACY IN ACTION!*

WE'LL WITNESS LIVE DEBATES! STUMP SPEECHES! ROBUST POLITICAL RHETORIC! THIS IS HISTORY IN THE MAKING! ISN'T IT *WONDERFUL?!!*

ARE THEY GONE YET?

SORRY, DAD. THE AMERICAN POLITICAL PROCESS HAS TO RUN IT'S COURSE!

SPRINGFIELD UNDER SIEGE: DAY 1

IF ANYONE WANTS ME, I'LL BE WHERE THE *ACTION* IS!

GOP MOBILE HEADQUARTERS

AH! THE GRAND OLD PARTY RUNNING AGAIN IN THE *GREAT RACE!* WHAT BETTER OPPORTUNITY FOR A LOYAL AND SLAVISH YOUNG SYCOPHANT LIKE MYSELF TO BE OF SERVITUDE TO AN ARCHAIC, WRINKLED, OLD CANDIDATE!

...THE SCENT OF MY EAGER CRAVENNESS MINGLED WITH THE AROMA OF HIS *TIMEWORN* LEADERSHIP!

KNOCK! KNOCK!

GOOD DAY, MY FRIEND! I'M HERE TO *OFFER* MY SERVICES AS A FAITHFUL PARTY FOLLOWER!

THAT'S GREAT, PAL! I'LL GIVE YOU AN ADDRESS WHERE YOU CAN SEND YOUR CHECK.

AH, WELL...YOU SEE, I'VE ALREADY MADE A SIZABLE CASH CONTRIBUTION. I'M HERE TO *VOLUNTEER* MY TIME AND ENERGY.

UH, NO THANKS, PAL. BUT KEEP THOSE CONTRIBUTIONS COMING!

I HAVE EXTENSIVE EXPERIENCE IN HANDLING INFIRM, YET *FORCEFUL*, ELDERLY GENTLEMEN. PERHAPS YOUR CANDIDATE IS IN NEED OF A SPONGE BATH? OR YOU HAVE SOME ENVELOPES THAT NEED LICKING?

SLAM!

DAMN *GROUPIES!*

WOW! IT'S JOE "DUKE" CANNON!

THE GREAT *RIGHT HOPE*! THE DEFENDER OF LIBERTY, JUSTICE AND THE AMERICAN WAY!

...AND SO WHERE DO I STAND ON THIS WHOLE "CRIME" THINGAMAJIGGY?

BASICALLY, SIR, YOU'RE FOR IT.

I'M *PRO-CRIME*?

WELL, NOT IN SO MANY WORDS, SIR. YOU SEE, THE MORE CRIME WE HAVE, THE MORE PRISONS WE BUILD, THE MORE GUARDS WE HIRE, THE MORE...

BASICALLY, SIR, *CRIME MEANS JOBS*.

YOU KNOW, "IT'S THE ECONOMY, STUPID."

ARE YOU TALKING TO ME?

AH, UM...IT'S AN EXPRESSION, SIR.

HMMM...AND MY OPPONENT? IS HE PRO-CRIME?

NO. BASICALLY, SIR, HE'S A WIMP.

A WIMP? OH, I LIKE *THAT*! I'M GONNA CALL HIM THAT!

"YOU, MY FRIEND, ARE A WIMP!"

RED ALERT! RED ALERT! WE GOT A CODE NINER-NINER! POSSIBLE TERRORIST SITUATION! REQUESTING BACK-UP.

HEY! *LET GO* OF ME!

SAY, HEY! WHAT'S ALL THE RUCKUS HERE?

SAM REASON! OUR ...UNTRY'S MOST *BELOVED* ...RESPECTED TELEVISION NEWSREADER!

HEE, HEE. I SEE YOU'VE BEEN READING USA TOADY! OFFICER, WHAT SEEMS TO BE THE PROBLEM?

I APPREHENDED THIS ALLEGED PER-PETRATOR ATTEMPTING A *BREAK-IN* OF MR. CANNON'S TRAILER.

NO WAY! I WAS JUST TRYING TO GET A FIRST-HAND LOOK AT A REAL, LIVE PRESIDENTIAL CANDIDATE.

WELL, WELL, WELL, LITTLE LADY. THEY REALLY DON'T COTTON TO MEMBERS OF THE GENERAL PUBLIC GETTING TOO CLOSE. MAKES EVERYBODY KINDA SKITTISH, YOU SEE.

BUT IF THE PUBLIC ISN'T ALLOWED NEAR THE CANDIDATES, HOW CAN WE DECIDE WHO TO VOTE FOR?

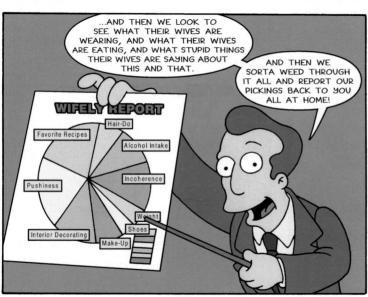

ARE THEY GONE YET?

NO, DAD! AND WHY HAS EVERYONE GONE INTO HIDING?

THIS IS OUR TOWN AND OUR COUNTRY! THE PEOPLE SHOULD BE OUT THERE ASKING THOSE CANDIDATES *TOUGH QUESTIONS* AND DEMANDING *REAL ANSWERS!*

BUT THEY FRIGHTEN US, HONEY! THEY TALK ABOUT *SCARY THINGS*...LIKE TAXES AND IMMIGRANTS!

THEY'VE *TAKEN OVER* THE WHOLE TOWN! I WISH THEY'D JUST LEAVE!

FORGET IT, MOM. IT LOOKS LIKE THEY'VE SETTLED IN.

WELL, THAT'S JUST GREAT! LOOK, THERE'S BEEN NOTHING BUT NEWS JUNK ON TV SINCE THEY GOT HERE.

...AND I WILL WORK TO EXPAND PRISON CAPACITY BY AS MUCH AS IT TAKES TO MAKE WHOEVER IS LEFT ON THE OUTSIDE FEEL SAFE!

AW, SHUT UP, YOU BIG WINDBAG!

WINDBAG?! HEE, HEE! I LIKE *THAT!* "YOU, SIR, ARE A *WINDBAG!*"

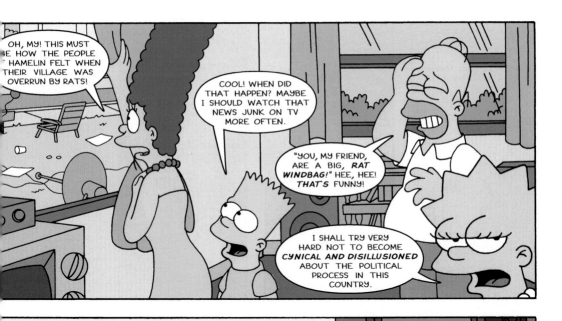

GOOD MORNING, AND WELCOME TO CMM'S "INSIDERS' CLUBHOUSE." I'M YOUR HOST, ED ANDERSON, AND JOINING ME ON TODAY'S PANEL...

DISTINGUISHED WASHINGTON COLUMNIST AND HARVARD LAW SCHOOL PROFESSOR, JACK WHITE...

HELLO, ED.

FAMOUS INTERNATIONAL CORRESPONDENT AND YALE ALUMNI, DAN SMITH...

'MORNING, ED.

AND NOTED NEWS COMMEN- TATOR AND FORMER ASSISTANT DEAN AT THE WHARTON SCHOOL OF ECONOMICS, HARRY ARMSTRONG...

'PLEASURE, ED.

TODAY'S TOPIC, GENTLEMEN, IS ONE YOU'RE ALL CERTAINLY WELL-QUALIFIED TO JUDGE: IS THE POLITICAL PROCESS IN THIS COUNTRY OUT OF TOUCH WITH THE AVERAGE, WORKING-CLASS AMERICAN?

JOIN US FOR PICKLED EGG NITE!

JACK?

I'D HAVE TO SAY NO, IT IS NOT, ED. AND I THINK WE HAVE *OURSELVES* TO THANK FOR THAT. THANKS TO TODAY'S EDUCATING MEDIA COVERAGE, PRESIDENTIAL CAMPAIGNING HAS TAKEN ON ALL THE *EXCITEMENT AND DRAMA* OF HORSE RACING!

AND WE EVEN *PICK THE WINNER* BEFORE THEY COME OUT OF THE GATE!

JACK'S RIGHT, ED! WE DISTILL THE CAMPAIGN DOWN INTO SIMPLE, FUN BITS THAT YOUR EVERYDAY, SIX-PACK KIND OF FELLOW CAN RELATE TO...

WE TAKE COMPLICATED ISSUES AND WEAVE THEM INTO COMPELLING POLITICAL NARRATIVES THAT MAKE THE VIEWER FEEL LIKE...

I'M GONNA PUKE! CAN YOU TURN THAT THING OFF, MOE?

OH, DEAR! I HOPE WE CAN FIND A STORE THAT'S OPEN!

LOOK, MOM! THE KWIK-E-MART!

...ARRIVING IN SPRINGFIELD TODAY, SENATOR JOHN "JOHN-JOHN" JOHNSON, COATLESS, WITH HIS SHIRT SLEEVES ROLLED UP, LOOKED READY TO TAKE HIS "UP WITH PEOPLE" MESSAGE DIRECTLY TO THE PEOPLE THEMSELVES...

HOLY COW!

IT'S SENATOR JOHN "JOHN-JOHN" JOHNSON! THE RICHEST, MOST HANDSOME MAN IN OUR NATION'S CAPITAL! THE BEST HAIRCUT INSIDE THE BELTWAY! THE "UP WITH PEOPLE" PEOPLE'S CHOICE AND MY OWN PERSONAL PRESIDENTIAL HOPEFUL!

HE'S SOOOOOOOO CUTE!

AWWW, CRIPES! I'M SO SICK OF THESE PLATITUDINOUS SMALL TOWN PHOTO-OPS!

I JUST HOPE YOU INCOMPETENT FOOLS HAVE LINED UP SOME DECENT WOMEN FOR TONIGHT! HOW MANY TIMES DO I HAVE TO TELL YOU IMBECILES--I'M NOT RUNNING FOR DOG-CATCHER!

UP WITH YOU, SENATOR!

AMID GROWING REPORTS THAT HE IS SIMPLY OUT OF TOUCH WITH MOST MIDDLE-CLASS AMERICANS, SENATOR JOHN "JOHN-JOHN" JOHNSON...

...IS CAMPAIGNING HARD TO DISTANCE HIMSELF FROM HIS LUCRATIVE, LIFELONG CAREER IN THE SENATE IN ORDER TO RE-INVENT HIMSELF AS A *MAN OF THE PEOPLE.*

...AND WE RAN OUT OF MILK DOWN AT CAMPAIGN HEADQUARTERS, SO I JUST POPPED OVER TO PICK UP A FIFTH, UH, A QUART OF...UM, MILK...

Duff
12.95
A CASE

OPEN 24 hrs

GEEZ, I'VE BEEN WATCHING THIS STUPID THING ALL DAY AND NOT ONE MENTION OF THAT RAT-INFESTED VILLAGE!

DO YOU KNOW THAT YOURS IS THE ONLY STORE OPEN IN TOWN?

YES, YES. OTHER CITIZENS OF YOUR GREAT COUNTRY FLEE LIKE MICE FROM YOUR GLORIOUS *SINKING SHIP OF STATE.* BUT NOT APU!

I WHOLLY EMBRACE YOUR OPEN AND SPIRITED ELECTION PROCESS, YOUR NARROW, YET COLORFUL POLITICAL SPECTRUM AND YOUR MAGNIFICENT FREE-MARKET SYSTEM, RIPE WITH THE BOUNTIFUL JOYS OF *PRICE-GOUGING* IN TIMES OF DIRE STATE AND LOCAL EMERGENCIES!

THAT WILL BE $23.50 FOR THE VERY SMALL JAR OF BABY FOOD, MUM.

SIVE

EEEEEEK!!!

OH, MY GOD!

LET'S SEE, OW...MILK, MILK...

UH, SENATOR? I BELIEVE THE MILK IS OVER THERE IN THE REFRIGERATOR CASE.

SEND THE BLUE-HAIRED BABE UP TO MY ROOM... BUT EIGHTY-SIX THE TODDLER.

UH, SENATOR... THAT'S NOT A CAMP FOLLOWER... IT'S JUST A LOCAL RESIDENT. WE HAVE NO IDEA HOW SHE GOT IN HERE.

YOU MORON! HOW MANY TIMES DO I HAVE TELL YOU IDIOTS: THE *AVERAGE CITIZEN* IS JUST A *WASTE OF MY TIME.*

BELIEVE ME, SENATOR, THE *FEELING IS MUTUAL!*

GOOD NIGHT!!! THESE POLITICIANS ARE SO REMOVED ROM US. WE'VE GONE FROM BEING MERELY *INCIDENTAL* TO BEING DOWNRIGHT *DISPENSABLE!*

HEY, DAD! GET A LOAD OF THIS GUY!

SURE. YOU GOT THE MEDIA TELLING YOU THAT I'M A NUTJOB. YOU GOT 'EM TELLING YOU I'M THE CANDIDATE FROM MARS... BUT LET ME TELL YOU, MR. AND MRS. AMERICA: *THE MEDIA LIES!* THEY TELL BIG, FAT, LIES! AND I'VE GOT THE *PIE CHARTS* TO PROVE IT!

INDEPENDENT CANDIDATE— L. RON PERCENT

AND THE PIE CHARTS *DO NOT LIE!* THE PIE CHARTS *CAN NOT LIE!* BECAUSE THE PIE CHARTS ARE FORBIDDEN BY *ZAROGG-3* TO TELL A LIE!!!

MMMMMMMMM... PIE CHARTS!

CAN YOU BELIEVE IT? I WAS *PERSONALLY INSULTED* BY A UNITED STATES SENATOR!

ALL RIGHT! WAY TO GO *MOM!*

THIS ENTIRE ELECTION IS A *CHARADE.* THE PEOPLE ARE *TOTALLY IRRELEVANT* TO THE PROCESS! IT'S A *FARCE!*

NOW, LISA, THERE'S NO NEED TO SWEAR.

CHOCO MIX

BUT DON'T YOU SEE, DAD? IT'S LIKE A CIRCUS THAT TRAVELS WITH ITS OWN AUDIENCE. THEY COME INTO TOWN AND PITCH A TENT AND PUT ON A SHOW, BUT NONE OF THE TOWNSPEOPLE ARE ALLOWED TO SEE IT.

THE TOWNSPEOPLE ONLY GET TO HEAR THE TRAVELING AUDIENCE'S AC- COUNT OF THE SHOW.

YEAH, CIRCUS...

DAD! WE, THE PEOPLE, ARE NEVER *ALLOWED* IN THE *TENT!!!*

BUT, LISA, HONEY... WE, THE PEOPLE, DON'T WANT TO GO *IN* THE TENT! IT'S A STUPID, BORING, SMELLY CIRCUS AND WE DON'T WANT TO SEE IT!

"Hi, Troy McClure here! You may remember me from such classic endorsements as 'Much Ado About Mu' 'What About Grout,' and 'Chinchillas: Your Rodent to Riches.' When I first called one of Krusty's psychic hadn't done a movie for over a year. I was broke, alone, and flabby, but she predicted I would soon be involved in a very high profile project. Not seven months later I landed a role in the heartwarming dram "A Fish Taco Called Juanita" with Cheech Marin! Since then, I've been hot, hot, hot! And it's all thanks to Krusty's Celebrity Psychic Hotline. Now here are some testimonials from other Krusty believers."

KRUSTYCO PRESENTS

KRUSTY'S CELEBRITY PSYCHIC HOTLINE

HI, EVERYBODY!
Dr. Nick Riviera here. I first consulted a Krusty Psychic because of concerns about the financial future of my elective surgery clinic. He described his vision of the clinic's success with six words: tanning beds, tanning beds, tanning beds! The next day I replaced our operating tables with state-of-the-art gas jet tanning grills! And now, what do you think? Liposuction, reconstruction, and a deep, dark, tropical tan – all in one visit! Business has never been better and it's all thanks to Krusty and his Celebrity Psychic Hotline.

HOLA MIS AMIGOS!
For an entertainer, the image is everything. So you can imagine my chagrin when I realized I had misplaced my bumblebee suit. Without the suit I am not a bee, I am... nothing. The world was as dark as the stripes on my beloved bee suit. The black stripes, not the yellow ones. Lucky for me, one of Krusty's psychics was only a phone call away. She told me to look "deep within" for the answer, and sure enough, a week later I found my suit deep within the trunk of my car!

GREETINGS, I'm Kent Brockman. Have you ever felt yo life was less than satisfying? I did, I called a Krusty Psychic. She told that I had a dream inside me, a dr that had to be set free like a little I broke down and confessed to her secret fantasy of being a rock st With her encouragement, I recorde album that just hit number one on German pop charts. Now I'm about star in a titillating new T.V. series o "Lifeguard Town" in which I play leader of a crack team of crimefig ing beach bunnies and ho-dads!

"As you can see, the key to your dreams is just a phone call away. So put your trusty in Krusty. He may be a clown, but his Celebrity Psychic Hotline is no joke."

FOR A LIMITED TIME ONLY!!! CALL NOW AND YOU WILL RECEIVE A VALUABLE GIFT!*

CALL NOW! 1-900-55-KRUST
$8.95 per minute**

*Choice of autographed picture of Krusty, autographed picture of Troy, autographed picture of Dr. Nick, autographed picture of Bumblebee Man, or a copy of Kent's CD, "Songs In The Key of Me." **Ten minute minimum

$8.95 rate with ten minute minimum applicable from 7:45am til 8:15am Tuesdays only. All other times $12.95 per minute, 45 minute minimum.

Krusty's Celebrity Psychic Hotline is a wholly owned subsidiary of KMRBB Enterprises, Krusty the Clown, Troy McClure, Dr. Nick Riviera, Bumblebee Man, Kent Brockman -- Directors.

MATT GROENING

MINUTE LATER...

⌣URP!⌢

MMMM... AFTERTASTE...

AHHHH, MR. ARM AND MR. HAMMER... I'VE SAVED THE BEST FOR LAST! THIS IS THE LIFE!

RELAXING ON THE SOFA WITH MY TWO BEST FRIENDS: *T.V.* **AND** *TASTY SNACK TREATS!* I'LL PROBABLY **NEVER** GET TO DO THIS WHEN I **GROW UP!**

COMING UP NEXT... "THE HOLLYWOOD SQUARES ON ICE!" FEATURING THE JUNE TAYLOR DANCERS!

ALL RIGHT! UMM... I'LL TAKE PAUL LYNDE, ON SKATES...TO BODY BLOCK.

THIS JUST IN... JAILBREAK AT FUZZ CENTRAL!

COBRA

THIS RIGHTEOUS, STONE COLD RADICAL HAS **FREED** HIMSELF FROM THE SHACKLES OF THE *ESTABLISHMENT OPPRESSION,* AND IS CRASHING SOMEWHERE IN BEAUTIFUL DOWNTOWN SPRINGFIELD.

LIKE, THERE'S A REWARD OF *FIVE THOUSAND* SIMOLEONS FOR INFORMATION THAT LEADS TO COBRA'S CAPTURE, BUT ANYONE WHO **RATS** ON HIM IS, IN **THIS** REPORTER'S OPINION, A **SELLOUT** TO THE MAN. FAR OUT, DUDES...

MMMMM... SIMOLEONS...

I'VE GOT A PLAN THAT'S GONNA GET ME SOME O' THEM!

AT LAST...MY MASTERPIECE! IF THAT COBRA GUY TRIES TO GET IN HERE HE'S TOAST ...MMMM, SMOTHERED WITH *SIMOLEON JELLY...*

AAAAAHHHH!!!

HE'S HERE! HE'S GONNA GET ME!

KNOCK! KNOCK!

H...H...HELLO...IS ANYBODY HOME?

HEY, THIS COBRA GUY SOUNDS LIKE A *PANTY WAIST*--I'M REALLY GONNA KICK SOME *BAD-GUY BUTT* NOW!

HI, I'M A LITTLE EAGLETTE! WOULD YOU BE INTERESTED IN BUYING MY COOKIES FOR A GOOD CAUSE?

COOKIES!!! NEXT TO DONUTS, THEY'RE MY *FAVORITE FOOD GROUP!*

PLINK!

FWOOSH!

MAKE ROOM, STOMACH! MR. CARAMEL CLUSTER'S GONNA PAY YOU A LITTLE VISIT!

SWISH!

CLACK!

WELCOME TO MY HOME, GIRL. ANYONE WHO HAS COOKIES IS A FRIEND OF MINE.

WHOOSH!

CHOP!

CREAK!

ENOUGH POLITENESS! NOW LEMME AT THOS GOOPITY-GOOEY, CRUNCH CARAMELEEEEEEE!!!

AAAAAHHHHH!!!!

D'OH!

MY TROOP LEADER WARNED ME... "STAY AWAY FROM THE HOUSE WITH THE *WEIRD LITTLE FAT KID,*" BUT I HADDA GO FOR MY *BRAVERY BADGE!*

OH BOY, YOU'VE DONE IT THIS TIME... CARAMEL CLUSTERS? HOW MANY TIME HAVE I TOLD YOU? GET THE THIN MINTS!

NO TABB FOR YOU!!

MUST...REACH... CLUSTERS! FATE OF STOMACH...HANGS IN...BALANCE...

Tabb

SCRIPT
CHRIS SIMMONS

PENCILS
SHAUN CASHMAN

INKS
TIM BAVINGTON

LETTERS
JEANNINE CROWELL

COLORS
NATHAN KANE

INNER CHILD
MATT GROENIN

...er, Barney & Moe in

E UNBEARABLE LIGHTNESS OF BARNEY

WHATSA MATTA, HOMER?

AW, NUTHIN' EXCITING EVER HAPPENS AROUND HERE, MOE.

WHADAYA MEAN NUTHIN' EVER HAPPENS? HOW 'BOUT THAT TIME MY SELTZER GUN GOT CLOGGED UP WITH LIME PULP?

YEAH, BUT THAT WAS LAST YEAR.

WHAT ABOUT WHEN I SWALLOWED THE EIGHT BALL?

YA DO THAT ALL THE TIME, BARN.

SEE? NOTHIN' EVER HAPPENS! *YOU* CLOG YOUR *SELTZER GUN, BARNEY* SWALLOWS THE *EIGHT BALL,* I GET MY TONGUE CAUGHT IN THE *CHANGE MACHINE...*

BARNEY'S BALL TAB

6 eight balls
3 cue balls
4 nine balls
6 chalk cubes
1 bowling pin

SAY, *I* KNOW, HOMER! WHY DON'T WE *MAKE* SOMETHN' HAPPEN!

NOW YOU'RE TALKIN'!

SNAP!

THAT ASSUMES WE INTRINSICALLY POSSESS ...E WILL. IF WE HAD *THAT,* WE PROBABLY ...ULDN'T EVEN BE *IN* HERE NOW; WHY, WE'D ...SEEING THE WORLD! *ITALY, GREECE, THE ...RTHENON, THE COLISSEUM!* AND THEN ...E COULD BUILD THINGS! AIR FIELDS! ...SKYSCRAPERS! BRIDGES A MILE LO--

UURRRP!

'NOTHER BEER, MOE.

ZZZ...

GAAH! HEY, THE *BEER TAP'S* CLOGGED! *THE BEER TAP'S CLOGGED!*

THE SAME OL' END.

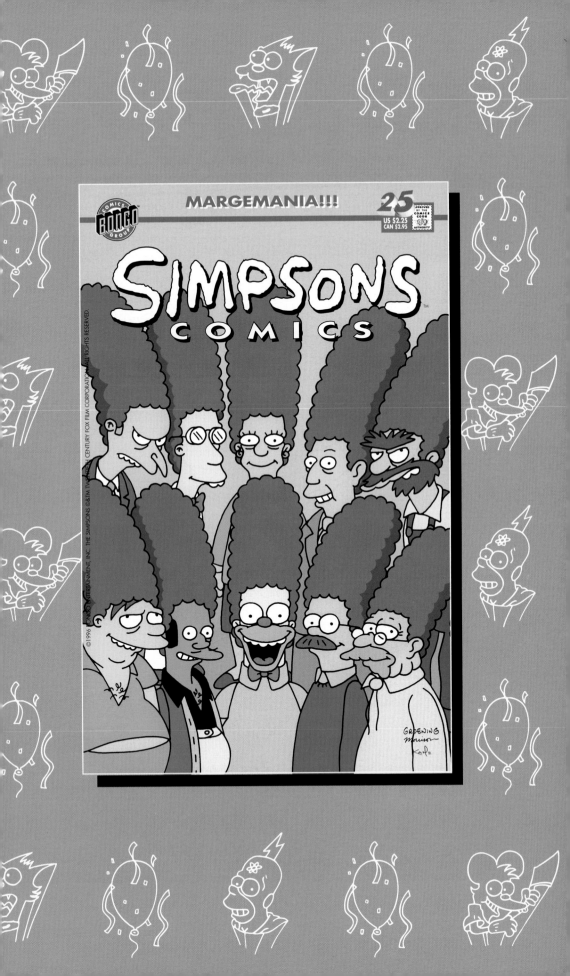

☆KENT☆ BROCKMAN

The Kent Brockman SHOW

WE'LL FIND OUT HOW THEIR FAMILIES FEEL ABOUT THESE MARSUPIAL MEN AND ASK THEM JUST WHAT *IT IS* THEY KEEP IN THOSE POUCHES AFTER THIS BREAK.

CAN WE PLEASE WATCH SOMETHING ELSE? THESE TALK SHOWS ARE VERY *UNAPPEALING* AND *DEGRADING*.

WHATEVER YOU SAY, MOM.

...THE SHAMELESS PRANKS AND HUMILIATIONS MEAN *NOTHING*...

CLICK!

...ONCE YOU'VE PARKED INSIDE ONE OF THOSE TINY CARS ON A MOONLIT NIGHT, YOU CAN NEVER GO BACK TO A *NORMAL MAN*.

CLICK!

WE'LL RETURN TO MEN WHO ENJOY HITTING TALK SHOW HOSTS WITH CHAIRS AFTER A WORD FROM-- ⸮YEEAGH!⸮

COOOL!

NO. TRY THE *EDUCATIONAL* STATION.

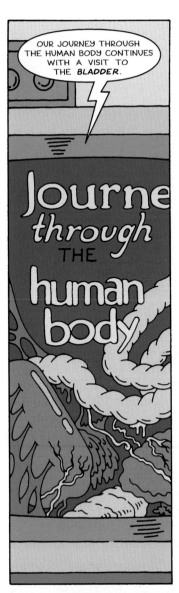

OUR JOURNEY THROUGH THE HUMAN BODY CONTINUES WITH A VISIT TO THE *BLADDER*.

Journey *through* THE human body

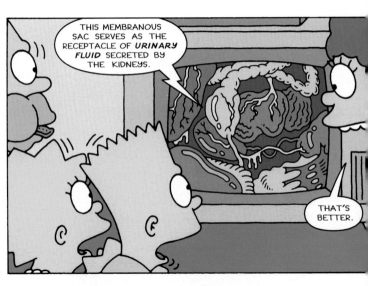

THIS MEMBRANOUS SAC SERVES AS THE RECEPTACLE OF *URINARY FLUID* SECRETED BY THE KIDNEYS.

THAT'S BETTER.

THE WALLS OF THE BLADDER CONSIST OF *UNSTRIPED SMOOTH MUSCULAR TISSUE* LINED BY A *MUCOUS MEMBRANE*.

WHEN MODERATELY DISTENDED, THE BLADDER IS ABOUT FIVE INCHES LONG AND THREE INCHES ACROSS...

...AND ORDINARILY CONTAINS ABOUT A *PINT* OF URINE.

ALRIGHT, ALRIGHT. CHANGE THE CHANNEL.

A FEW DAYS LATER AT QUIMBY CAMPAIGN HEADQUARTERS...

IF YOU WANT TO GENERATE ENTHUSIASM, YOU'RE GONNA NEED SOMETHING A LITTLE MORE *HARD-HITTING*.

OUR SURVEYS INDICATE THAT MOST SPRINGFIELDIANS *ALREADY* CALL THIS TOWN SPRINGFIELD.

SOOO, AH, WHAT ABOUT THE FOLKS THAT, AH, *DON'T* CALL THIS TOWN SPRINGFIELD?

WE BELIEVE THOSE VOTERS *KNOW* THAT THE NAME OF THE TOWN *IS* SPRINGFIELD, MAYOR...

...BUT FOR SOME QUAINT REASONS OF THEIR OWN THEY INSIST ON REFERRING TO IT AS "THE HELLHOLE" INSTEAD.

YOU'VE GOT TO FIND A HOT-BUTTON ISSUE TO ATTACK, SOMETHING THAT PEOPLE WILL *RALLY* AROUND.

SLAM!

HOW ABOUT THE OIL COMPANIES OR TRIAL LAWYERS? *EVERYONE* HATES THEM.

WE CAN'T GO AFTER THEM. THEY'RE OUR BIGGEST CAMPAIGN CONTRIBUTORS.

I'VE *GOT* IT! *EVERYONE* HATES IT WHEN THEY FORGET WHERE THEY PUT THEIR KEYS, RIGHT?

RIGHT. SOOO?

SO. WE GO AFTER *THEM!*

WHAAP!

WE GO AFTER THE PEOPLE WHO FORGET THEIR KEYS?

PRECISELY!

I THINK I'VE FOUND OUR ANSWER RIGHT *HERE*, PEOPLE.

ELECT JOE QUIMBY

LATER THAT DAY...

SO, MARGE, THE MAYOR IS IN *COMPLETE AGREEMENT* WITH YOU. HE, TOO, BELIEVES PEOPLE'S PRIVATE LIVES ARE BEST KEPT TO *THEMSELVES* AND *OUT OF THE PUBLIC EYE*. ISN'T THAT *RIGHT*, MAYOR?

QUIMB

MAYOR?

SLAP!

I AM IN, ER, AH, *TOTAL AGREEMENT* WITH YOU.

SO, MRS. SIMPSON, HERE'S WHAT WE'D LIKE TO DO...

I ♥ QUIMBY

XT DAY AT THE TV STUDIO...

WHEN WE COME BACK, WE'LL TALK TO PEOPLE WHOSE LIVES HAVE BEEN RUINED BY *TALK SHOWS*.

YOU'LL DO THE SHOW AND *LIKE IT* "BROCKMAN," UNLESS YOU WANT THE VIEWING PUBLIC TO LEARN WHAT YOUR NAME *REALLY* IS.

NO! I'LL DO IT. IF THEY WERE TO FIND OUT MY NAME IS *BROCK KENTMAN*--

THEY JUST MIGHT START ASKING WHY.

I THOUGHT THAT CONFESSING ON TV WOULD *PURGE MY SOUL* AND *FREE ME*, BUT NOW EVEN THE CHILDREN MAKE FUN OF ME...

BUT DON'T YOU FEEL BETTER *NOW* HAVING TOLD US THIS. SURELY IT *HELPS YOU* TO TELL US ABOUT THIS.

I WISH I'D NEVER SAID *ANYTHING!*

TOOTY-TOOT-TOOT!

HAW HAW!

THIS IS *EMBARRASSING*. PEOPLE USED TO HAVE A SENSE OF *GUILT* ABOUT THESE THINGS. NOW THEY JUST GO OUT AND TALK ABOUT IT TO EVERYONE.

HUH?

BUT CAN'T YOU FEEL HER *PAIN*, MRS. SIMPSON?

PEOPLE CAN DO WHAT THEY WANT, BUT DO THEY HAVE TO TELL US ABOUT IT? WE DON'T WANT TO KNOW. PEOPLE IN GLASS HOUSES SHOULD ALWAYS WEAR CLOTHES.

YE-YAS!

RIGHT ON!

YES!

SPEAK IT!

CIVILIZATION DEPENDS ON KEEPING *CERTAIN THINGS* UNDER WRAPS. THERE'S CLEARLY AN *UNDERSIDE TO HUMANITY,* BUT IT'S A LITTLE *WEIRD* WHEN YOU START CELEBRATING THE WORST THINGS IN *PUBLIC.*

THERE'S SUCH A THING AS *"CONSTRUCTIVE HYPOCRISY"* -- NOT TELLING EVERYTHING YOU KNOW [IN] ORDER TO PRESERVE THE HIGHER GOOD. IT'S [IM]PORTANT TO IMPART A *WHOLESOME IMAGE* [T]O SOCIETY, EVEN IF IT MEANS *LEAVING OUT* THINGS THAT ARE *TRUE.*

OWWW!

[HE]AR, HEAR!

OH NO! I'LL *NEVER* GET THAT, AH, STAIN OUT. MY SUIT IS *RUINED!*

NO, IT'S NOT.

THERE YOU GO!

HEY, CHIEF, DID YOU GET A LOAD OF *THAT?*

YUP. THAT'S *MIGHTY GOOD CLEANING,* BOYS. GET THE TV STATION ON THE HORN AND FIND OUT *HOW* SHE DID THAT.

YES, MOTHER, I *KNOW* HER CHILDREN GO TO SCHOOL HERE, BUT THAT DOESN'T MEAN SHE KNOWS HOW TO GET SARSAPARILLA OUT OF A *TAFFETA BUSTLE*--UH HUH...UH HUH...YES, MOTH-- UH HUH...I'M SORRY. I'LL CALL THE STATION *RIGHT AWAY.*

THAT'S ABSOLUTELY *STAIN-TASTIC!*

ALRIGHT, MOM!

MMMMM... STAINS.

THE NETWORK PRESIDENT'S OFFICE...

THAT SHOW GENERATED THE *BIGGEST FLURRY OF CALLS* WE'VE EVER RECEIVED.

BUT--

NETWORK PRESIDENT

YES, BROCKMAN, I KNOW. THERE'S THAT CUTE LITTLE FOREST PIG THAT GAVE BIRTH TO *TWINS*, BUT WE CAN'T COUNT ON THAT HAPPENING EVERY DAY. BROCKMAN, *YOU'RE FIRED!*

GET ME *MARGE SIMPSON!*

AND SOON...

...IT WAS ONLY A LITTLE *BENZINE* MIXED WITH *BROCCOLI WATER.* IT'S WHAT'S LEFT OVER AFTER YOU STEAM THE BROCCOLI. I ALWAYS CARRY SOME WITH ME.

MY OWN SHOW? I WOULDN'T KNOW WHAT TO DO!

MOM...JUST TWO WORDS: *STREET LUGE* AND EXPLOSIONS--LOTS OF EXPLOSIONS.

...SINCE *MY* DAY, THE *OPPORTUNITIES* FOR SEVERE BONE TRAUMA AND PENETRATING LACERATIONS HAVE INCREASED *ENORMOUSLY!*

BLAM!

KA-POW

DONUTS ARE THE ANSWER, MARGE.

THEY'LL MAKE ALL YOUR GUESTS *HAPPY AS CLAMS.*

JUST *BE* OURSELF, MOM.

BACK AT CAMPAIGN HEADQUARTERS...

THESE ARE THE *WORST APPROVAL RATINGS* I'VE SEEN SINCE 1972, WHEN *NIXON* BEAT OUT *CHUCK BARRIS* FOR THE MOST HATED AND FEARED MAN IN HISTORY. IT'S NOT *HOPELESS*; HOWEVER, LOOK AT HIM *TODAY.* NIXON'S NEVER BEEN *MORE POPULAR!*

BUT, ER, AH, *NIXON'S DEAD!*

BELIEVE ME, WE *SERIOUSLY CONSIDERED* THAT OPTION.

BUT WE THINK IF YOU GRAB ONTO THIS *MARGE SIMPSON ANGLE,* THINGS WILL START TO LOOK UP.

HUH?

WAIT HERE, I'LL INTRODUCE YOU.

HELLO, MY DEAR!

...FURTHER ADO, *MAYOR DIAMOND JOE QUIMBY!*

POP!

I'D JUST LIKE TO SAY THAT IN, AH, HONOR OF *MARGE SIMPSON* AND BY THE AUTHORITY VESTED IN ME, I DECLARE THIS DAY, "*CONSTRUCTIVE HYPOCRISY DAY.*"

LATER AT THE TV STATION...

YOU'RE VERY *KIND*. THANK YOU. THIS IS A *NEW EXPERIENCE* FOR ME, AND I MUST ADMIT I REALLY DIDN'T KNOW WHAT TO DO, BUT MY DAUGHTER, LISA, SAID JUST BE YOURSELF...

SO, *HERE* I AM!

CLAP! CLAP! CLAP! CLAP!

WOW! I NEVER KNEW THE CARPET WAS SUPPOSED TO BE *THIS COLOR!*

:SNIFF: I MISS MY SOFA.

DON'T WORRY, HOMEBOY...

...WHEN MOM'S A *STAR* WE'LL ALL GET *NEW SOFAS!*

COOOL!

THE *FIRST* THING I'D LIKE TO DO IS SHARE A RECIPE FOR ONE OF MY *FAVORITE DESSERTS*...

HAH! YOU CALL *THIS* ENTERTAINMENT?

...AND MAYOR QUIMBY HAS *KINDLY*, THOUGH *SOMEWHAT ODDLY*, INSISTED ON HELPING OUT.

SHORT TIME LATER...

...ONCE THE HORSERADISH PLUMMETS TO THE BOTTOM, THE BOILING GELATIN IS READY TO BE POURED INTO THE MOLDS. BUT FIRST WE HAVE TO ADD *ONE MORE THING*...

DONNY

MARIE

TV

...A *SMILE!*

SEE?

THE EXTRA INGREDIENT IS *NICENESS*! COME ON, MAYOR QUIMBY, *SMILE* AT YOUR *GELATIN!*

CLAP!

CLAP!

THIS FEELS, AH, *FOOLISH*.

IT'S VERY *NICE*.

IT'S NOT FAIR. BY RIGHTS ALL THIS *TAWDRY PUBLICITY* AND, ER, *MEANINGLESS FAME* SHOULD BE *MINE! MINE I TELL YOU!*

SMASH!

VAGUE

CHIPS

SNACKS

I KNOW!

HEH, HEH, HEH, HEH. THAT DEADBEAT PHOTOGRAPHER HAD *NO IDEA* WHAT HE HAD ON THIS FILM!

KLAK KLAK

AAAND...OFF GOES THE *BAD HEAD*, ON GOES THE *BLUE HEAD*. HEE, HEE, HEE! WHEN THIS *DOCTORED PHOTO* HITS THE PAPERS, THE BEAUTY THAT IS BROCKMAN WILL *LIVE AGAIN!*

BACK AT THE PLANT...

LOOKING GOOD THERE, HOMER.

BOY, *I'LL SAY!*

KNOCK IT OFF, GUYS. THIS WAS THE ONLY THING IN THE HOUSE THAT WAS *CLEAN!*

IT'S NOT *THAT,* HOMER. IT'S YOUR COLORING. I JUST ALWAYS THOUGHT OF YOU AS AN *AUTUMN.*

HA-HA-HA-HA!!!

HOO-HOO!

PERHAPS THESE SUMMER HUES *HAVE* LOST THEIR ALLURE.

AT SPRINGFIELD ELEMENTARY...

THE LUNCH HOMER MAKES IS *BAD ENOUGH*...

...BUT I REALLY HATE THE WAY HE *PACKS* IT.

≡GURK≡ HOW CAN YOU STAND IT?

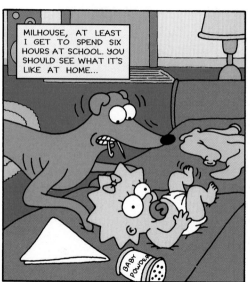

MILHOUSE, AT LEAST I GET TO SPEND SIX HOURS AT SCHOOL. YOU SHOULD SEE WHAT IT'S LIKE AT HOME...

BABY POWDER

AND, BACK AT QUIMBY HQ...

WELL, QUIMBY, IT LOOKS LIKE YOU AND A LADY FRIEND HAVE MADE THE SCANDAL SHEETS *AGAIN*.

The National Satellite

DON'T WORRY. I'VE GOT, AH, *ALIBIS* THAT CAN PUT ME IN *HALF A DOZEN* DIFFERENT PLACES AT ANY TIME.

WAIT A MINUTE! I NEVER HAD *ANYTHING* TO DO WITH *MARGE SIMPSON*. THIS WILL *RUIN* MY REPUTATION! SHE'S NOT *MY TYPE*!!

QUI

PRECISELY. WHICH COULD BE *JUST WHAT WE NEED* TO PUT YOU OVER THE TOP.

MARGE

PLAY IT UP, QUIMBY. *PLAY IT UP!*

LATER, AT THE STATION...

OH MY GOODNESS! IT'S THAT *CAMPAIGN WORKER*. IF SHE'S IN ON THIS, I'LL *NEVER* CLEAR MY GOOD NAME...

THE NATIONAL INQUISITOR

WELL, THE *BOUVIER* FAMILY NAME, ANYWAY. I GUESS I'LL HAVE TO CALL HER.

LATER THAT DAY, BROADCASTING LIVE...

NOW FOLKS, IT'S THAT TIME WHERE WE MAKE SOME *STAINS* GO AWAY.

WHAT IS THE MEANING OF THESE FLOWERS, MAYOR QUIMBY?

THE STAINIAC 3000

I THINK YOU KNOW, *MARGE*.

ARE YOU SAYING THESE *TABLOID RUMORS* ABOUT US ARE *TRUE*?

PEOPLE DON'T WANT TO KNOW ABOUT OUR, AH, *PRIVATE LIVES*, MARGE.

WE DON'T *HAVE* ANY PRIVATE LIFE. AND DON'T CALL ME "*MARGE*."

OH...I, AH, GET IT. "CONSTRUCTIVE HYPOCRISY," RIGHT, *MRS. SIMPSON*?

LADIES AND GENTLEMEN, I MUST *APOLOGIZE* FOR WHAT I AM ABOUT TO DO. I REALLY HATE IT! IT'S SO UNAPPEALING AND DEGRADING. HOWEVER, THE MAYOR HAS LEFT ME *NO CHOICE*. AND I'VE DISCOVERED THAT THE TRUTH IS *WORTH* STOOPING FOR, NO MATTER HOW *LOW YOU GO*.

WELL, MAYOR QUIMBY, SINCE IT SEEMS YOU'RE ANXIOUS TO HAVE EVERYONE BELIEVE YOU'RE INVOLVED WITH SOMEONE YOU'RE NOT, YOU WON'T OBJECT TO OUR *SURPRISE GUEST!*

OUR VIEWERS MIGHT *ECOGNIZE* HER FROM THIS *PICTURE!*

MAYOR QUIMBY HAS NOT ONLY *BETRAYED* THIS YOUNG LADY AND MYSELF, BUT HIS *SLEAZY ELECTIONEERING* HAS SULLIED THE VERY NAME OF SPRINGFIELD ITSELF.

OH MY!

BIG DEAL.

I DON'T, AH, ER, H, THINK THE PUBLIC NEEDS TO KNOW ABOUT THIS.

WHY DON'T WE LET *THEM* DECIDE?

YAAAAY!!

YES!

I ♥ QUIMBY

THWAK!

IND YOUR OWN TAIN REMOVER. *I QUIT!!!*

THE STAINIAC 3000

TEE-HEE.

YAAAAY!!

GO MARGE!

ALRIGHT!

YES!

YAY!

WOO-HOO!

YAY, MOM!

GROOVY STAIN!

SOME WEEKS LATER...

...WHEN I FOUND OUT SHE WAS SEEING THIS *CLOWN*, IT MADE ME *HOPPING MAD*.

KENT AND I WILL BE RIGHT BACK WITH *MORE SHAMELESS REVELATIONS* AFTER THIS.

WHAT THE PUBLIC *WANTS*, THE PUBLIC *DESERVES*.

THEY CAN *BROADCAST IT*, BUT I DON'T HAVE TO *WATCH IT!*

CLICK!

THE

12:47 PM

NOBODY BEATS OUR BLINTZES!

THAT'S GOOD PIE.

YUP.

12:48 PM

NOBODY BEATS OUR BLINTZES!

CLIK!

HEY, I THINKS THAT'S MY *PANCREAS* ON THE FLOOR! *HEY,* TINY, GIVE IT ALL *HERE!*

YEEEHAUGHK!!!

KERSMASH

1:01 PM

NOBODY BEATS OUR BLINTZES!

METER'S EXPIRED. SOME DAYS THIS JOB NEVER ENDS.

TAKE IT EASY, LOU. THIS TIME IT'S ON ME...

WHOOPS, LOOKS LIKE I'M OUTTA CHANGE. CALL IT IN.

1:26 PM

BEATS OUR BLINTZES!

SPRINGFIELD TIRE AND TOW

...BUT I WAS *HELD UP* AT THE BANK.

I MEAN, FIRST I WAS WAITING IN LINE FOR HALF AN HOUR AND THEN *THE BANK* WAS HELD UP! PLEASE...

OVER A

TERRY DELEGEANE
SCRIPT

PHIL ORTIZ
PENCILS

TIM BAVINGTON
INKS

NATHAN KANE
COLORS

CHRIS UNGAR
LETTERS

MATT GROEN
STEADY CUST

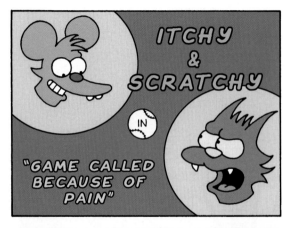

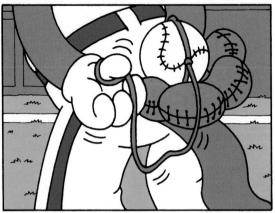

SCRIPT
JAMIE ANGELL

PENCILS
PHIL ORTIZ

INKS
TIM BAVINGTON

LETTERS
JEANNINE CROWELL

COLORS
NATHAN KANE

BEACH BALL CONFISCA
MATT GROENING

PLOP!

FWAP!

DINK!

K-RAK!

JOHN 3:16

VISITORS

YOINK!

VISITORS | 1 3 4
HOME | 0 0 0 0

SMACK!

THE END.

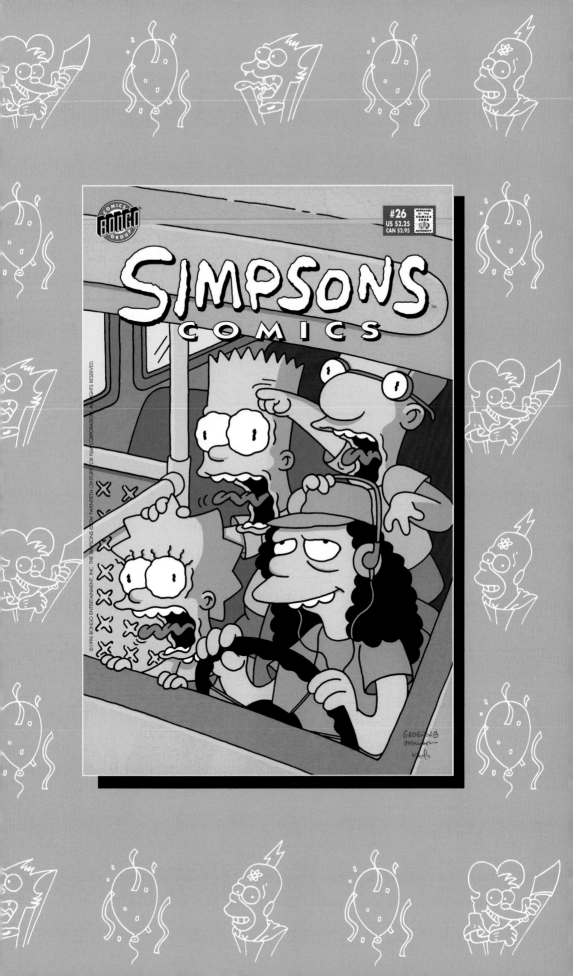

TIE A YELLOW RIBBON 'ROUND THAT OLD OAK TREE!

BLASTED MAGAZINE SUBSCRIPTION CARDS!

CONTROLLING YOUR ANGER WEEKLY

RING-A-RING!

THE PHRASE THAT PAYS IS "OLDIES DON'T MAKE ME MOLDY ON KBOR-FM." *DID* I *WIN*?!

ONLY IF *WINNING* MEANS SENDING HUNDREDS OF STUDENTS TO THEIR *UNTIMELY DEATH*.

BUT WHAT ABOUT THE DREAM DATE WITH *DIONNE WARWICK*?

YOU DON'T UNDERSTAND. I'M CALLING TO *WARN* YOU ABOUT YOUR *SCHOOL BUSES*.

IF THEY ARE NOT *IMMEDIATELY* EQUIPPED WITH THE PROPER SAFETY FEATURES, SOMEONE IS GOING TO GET *SERIOUSLY INJURED*!

LISTEN, YOU COMMIE, BLEEDING HEART ACTIVIST, THOSE BUSES HAVE BEEN RUNNING FINE SINCE 1936. IF YOU THINK I'M GOIN TO TAKE MONEY FROM THIS SCHOOL'S PRECIOUS TRANSPORTATION-FACULTY SNACK FUND, YOU'RE *NUTS*!

I *IMPLORE* YOU TO HEED MY WARN THE LIVES OF YO STUDENTS ARE AT RISK!

LISTEN PAL, I THINK SOME ENDANGERED TREE SNAILS IN SOUTH AMERICA COULD USE YOUR BLEEDING HEART. WHY DON'T YOU FLY DOWN THERE AND SAVE *THEM*?!

PRINCIPAL SKINNER, [B]ART SIMPSON WAS [R]UNNING AROUND OUR CLASSROOM *NUDE!*

WELL, SIMPSON, YOU'VE HAD QUITE A WEEK. KETCHUP PACKS UNDER THE FACULTY TOILET SEATS, SEA MONKEYS IN THE SWIMMING POOL AND NOW THIS, THIS...*PUBLIC DISPLAY OF NUDITY!*

SLAM!

I COULDN'T HELP IT. MY CLOTHES FELL OFF... IT WAS BAD STITCHING... I FORGOT MY BELT... I'M A VICTIM OF GRAVITY!

MISTER, I WOULD SAY YOUR SHENANIGANS HAVE EARNED YOU AN ENTIRE DAY *NOT* AT THE WATER PARK. YOU'LL REMAIN LOCKED IN THIS OFFICE ALL DAY TO THINK ABOUT WHAT YOU'VE DONE WHILE EVERYONE ELSE GOES ON THE FIELD TRIP...

AW, *MAN!*

...MS. KRABAPPEL, I'VE INSTRUCTED [O]TTO TO GO AHEAD WHILE YOU AND I STOP AT *MY* HOUSE. MOTHER FORGOT TO PACK MY *WATER WINGS.*

THIS IS *PREPOSTEROUS!* BEING *SPURNED* BY THE VERY INSTITUTION I'M TRYING TO *HELP!*

AND WHAT IS *THIS?* "EL BARTO." COULD THIS BE THE *SEAT* OF MY LOATHSOME, NE'ER-DO-WELL NEMESIS, *BART SIMPSON?*

El Barto

KRUSTY BAR

AHH-HA-HA-HA-HA!!! REVENGE IS SO SWEET WHEN IT'S SERVED WITH A LITTLE SIDE OF *MURDER!*

[A]ND SOON...

AND, OH, IF THAT IGNORANT PRINCIPAL HAD ONLY *LISTENED...* WHEN THIS BUS PULLS TO A STOP, YOUNG MASTER SIMPSON'S SEAT WILL SPRING FORWARD, MAKING BART A SPECTACULAR, SCREAMING ADVERTISEMENT FOR THE IMPORTANCE OF PROPER SAFETY RESTRAINTS.

El Barto

IF FOUND RETURN TO SPRINGFIELD PENITENTIARY TORTURE CHAMBER.

HAH! I'M KILLING *TWO BIRDS WITH ONE BUS!*

HEY, MAN, IS MY BUS READY? I GOTTA CRUISE THOSE KIDS TO THE WATER PARK. THEN I'M GONNA CATCH ME SOME RIGHTEOUS RAYS.

OH, IT'S *READY* ALRIGHT. HAVE A GOOD TIME... AND TELL MY FRIEND BART TO HAVE A WONDERFUL *SPRING* AND EVENTUAL *FALL!* BWA-HA-HA!!

UH, YEAH... WILL DO.

MOMENTS LATER...

ALL I NEED IS A PICTURE FRAME, TWO HANGERS, SOME DENTAL FLOSS AND THIS LADDER.

THAT'LL WORK.

CRASH!

SORRY, DUDE, BUT I'M GOING TO HAVE TO *COMMANDEER THIS VEHICLE!* HEH, HEH!

BUMP!

I THINK IT'S TIME FOR A QUICK TRIP AROUND THE WORLD.

KLA-CHAK!

99 BOTTLES OF DUFF ON THE WALL! 99 BOTTLES OF DUFF!

IF ONE OF THOSE BOTTLES SHOULD HAPPEN TO FALL...

HOLY COW, LOOK AT THAT KID! *THAT'S INCREDIBLE!*

HEY, MORON, FOR THE 8,723RD TIME, WHEN *YOU* LOOK *UP*, *I* LOOK *DOWN*. I CAN'T SEE *SQUAT!*

THIS IS ARNIE PIE IN THE SKY SAYING ALL'S CLEAR ON THE NORTHBOUND INTERSTATE, EXCEPT FOR A *FLYING BOY* WHO'S ATTACKING MY *CHOPPER!*

BRING HER ON IN, ARNIE. IT'S TIME FOR YOUR MEDICATION.

YAAAAHHH!

KRUMPF!

YAKOOOMF!

OTTO, MAN, SOMEONE'S RIGGED THIS BUS WITH A *BOMB!* IF YOU GO UNDER 55 MPH THE BUS WILL *BLOW!*

COOL!

ORDINARILY, I WOULD AGREE WITH YOU, BUT IN THIS CASE.. *WE COULD ALL DIE!*

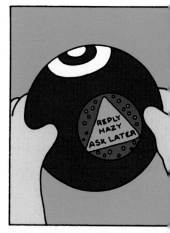

...EWHERE...

CALLING ALL CARS! WE HAVE A 563 ON THE NORTHBOUND INTERSTATE. OVER.

I SAID *WALK* THE STRAIGHT LINE, NOT *PASS OUT AND DROOL* ON IT!

ZZZZZZZ...;BURP;...
ZZZZZZZZZ...;BURP;

A 563!! GET THE *KAYAKS,* BOYS! WE GOT A *TIDAL WAVE* COMIN' THROUGH!!

NO, A 563 MEANS HOOKER WITH A GRENADE LAUNCHER.

ISN'T 563 THE NUMBER FOR THE PU PU PLATTER AT WANG'S SZECHUAN COTTAGE?!

HELP! BOMB ON BUS!

A 563 *AND* A BOMB BUS?!! LOOKS LIKE WE'LL BE EARNIN' OUR PAY TODAY, BOYS.

ATTENTION, PUPILS. *DO NOT PANIC.* WE HAVE *THREE* OPTIONS. *FIRST,* YOU NEED TO *STOP THE BUS!*

IF WE SLOW DOWN, THE BOMB WILL GO OFF!

OKAY, DO YOU KNOW HOW TO DEFUSE A BOMB?

NO. WHAT'S THE *THIRD* THING?

NO CLUE. I WAS KIND OF HOPING THE FIRST TWO WOULD WORK.

THIS JUST IN--A SCHOOL BUS REPORTEDLY CARRYING 90 TONS OF TNT, SIX M-80S AND SEVERAL ROLLS OF CAPS IS HEADED STRAIGHT FOR *DOWNTOWN SPRINGFIELD*.

HIGHWAY TO HELL

Kent

WE GO TO OUR EXCLUSIVE CHANNEL 6 *COP-CAM* TO PUT YOU AS *CLOSE* TO THE ACTION AS *HUMANLY POSSIBLE*.

COP CAM

CAN'T GET COMFY...*HEY,* WHO LEFT THE GUN ON THE SEAT AGAIN?

EXCLUSIVE

OH, MY GOSH! THAT'S BART AND LISA DRIVING THAT BUS!

YOU SEE MARGE? I'M NOT THE *ONLY* ONE WHO GETS HIS HAND STUCK IN THE 8-TRACK!

LISA, CAN YOU KEEP IT UNDER CONTROL?

I CAN DO *FINE* AS LONG AS THERE'S *NO TRAFFIC!*

WELCOME TO **SPRINGFIELD** TRAFFIC CAPITAL OF THE WORLD

MAN, THAT COULD HAVE BEEN *REALLY* EXPENSIVE.

YEAH.

AND THE WINNER OF THE *FINE CHINA STACKING CON-TEST* IS--

HONK HONK!!

Ned Flanders

WELL POLISH MY PICKLE PLATE! BY PROCESS OF ELIMIN-ATION, *WE'RE* THE VICTORS!

Ned Flanders

KA-RASH!

THAT WAGON ISN'T STOPPING!

FLOOR IT! CUTTING THEM OFF IS OUR ONLY CHANCE!!

C'MON HORSEY! LE'S BEAT THAT BUS! C'MON HORSEY!

HOLD ON, EVERYBODY!! WE'RE GOIN' THROUGH!!!

CRASH!!

LOOK, BRANDINE! WE'RE ON A BUS!

YOR DREAM HAS FINALLY COME TRUE.

MEANWHILE...

HA-HA-HA!

MY PLAN IS BEING EXECUTED TO A "T."

IT IS ONLY A MATTER OF TIME BEFORE THEY HAVE TO DROP BELOW 55 MPH AND BART SIMPSON WILL BE *FLUNG* TO HIS WELL-OVERDUE *DEMISE!*

KILL BART!

WHEW, THAT WAS CLOSE.

THREE DAYS LATER...

MEDALS, PUBLIC ADORATION, AMNESTY FOR THE BEING NAKED IN CLASS THING... I COULD GET USED TO BEING A HERO.

I DON'T KNOW, BART. THIS WHOLE THING SMACKS OF A CHEAP POLITICAL PHOTO-OP.

MMM,BOY PIZZA

WHO CARES? THERE'S FREE PIZZA!

LADIES AND GENTLEMEN...

IF THIS NEAR TRAGEDY HAS TAUGHT US ANYTHING, IT IS THAT OUR SCHOOL BUSES ARE SORELY *LACKING* IN SAFETY...

YES! YES! DESPITE ALL, THEY'VE HEARD MY CALL! THESE ADDITIONAL SEVENTY YEARS OF INCARCERATION WILL NOT BE FOR NAUGHT!

...THAT IS WHY WE HAVE INSTALLED A BASIC PROTECTIVE MEASURE TO ENSURE THE WELL-BEING OF EVERY STUDENT OF OUR BELOVED SPRINGFIELD ELEMENTARY!

THE EMERGENCY EJECTOR TOP!

NOW, WHEN A CHILD SENSES DANGER, THEY CAN IMMEDIATELY GRAB THE PATENTED DANGER CORD, AND...

WHAM!

THE ROOF GONE, CHILDREN CAN NOW SAFELY JUMP OUT OF THE RUNAWAY VEHICLE!

WELL, LOOKY THAT!

HOORAY!!

WAITAMINUTE--

NOW *THAT'S* A PRECAUTION!!

MY CAR!!!

D'OH!

END OF THE L

TALES OF THE BRINY DEEP

Featuring CAPTAIN McCALLISTER in "DOWN THE HATCHES BOYS"

PLEASE BRING ME MY *MACKEREL!*

AWWW...WELL, MA'AM. YOU SEE, IT'S... SAY, LADDIE! DID YE EVER HEAR THE WAY I CAME BY ME PEG LEG?

PEG LEG? *COOL!*

ZAHRRR! MISSUS, I DON'T MIND TELLIN' THE BOY. I WERE MUCH RIPER IN YEARS THAN THIS YOUNG FELLA WHEN I W SHANGHAIED AS CABIN BOY ONTO THE SCUMMIEST TUB T SIDE OF DAVY JONES'S LOCKER. *THE "INSIPID"* AS S WERE CALLED, WAS FREIGHTED TO THE GILLS WIT WHATNOT, BOUND FOR WHO KNOWS, CREWED B THE FLOTSAM OF EVERY SEEDY DOWN-IN-THE-DUMP PORT O' CALL--HARD-BOILED CUTTHROATS AND WIZENED OLD WHARF RATS ALL.

MY *MACKEREL,* PLEASE!

IT WERE NOT *ALL* BAD, HOWEVER, WHEN WE GOT OUR WEEKLY RATION OF CHEER--EACH MAN, A FULL PANNIKIN OF *SQUISHEE!* WE'D DANCE LIKE DERVISHES, KEEPING TIME TO THE GROAN OF THE ROPES AND SPARS. CURLY BOY'S SQUEEZEBOX KEPT US ALL JUMPING LIKE MONKEYS, IT DID. THOUGH THIS WERE NOT SOMETHING THE *CAP'N* MUCH SMILED UPON.

CAPTAIN'S QUARTERS

"SQUISH-EES MADE ME GO TO SEA, SQUISH-EES, JOHNNY, SQUISH-EES BOUGHT AND SQUISHEES FREE, SQUISH-EES FOR MY JOHNNY."

BOY, FETCH MY VICTUALS FROM THE COOK. YOU MEN! *BELA* THAT BEJABBERIN' AN SING SOMETHING MORE *CIVILIZED!*

I HUSTLED BELOW DECKS WHERE I ENCOUNTERED THE COOK UP TO HER NECK IN WORK.

"PUFF THE MAGIC DRAGON, LIVED BY THE SEA..."

POT

TOE

POTATOE

WAS ABOUT TO ROUSE HER, WHEN THE ~~ERCEST~~ AND MOST **BLOODCURDLINGEST** ~~UND~~ A SAILOR CAN HEAR SAVED ME ~~E~~ TROUBLE.

DIII-DULLL-EEEEE!!!

WE'D BEEN BOARDED BY *PIRATES!* 'TWERE THE MOST BLOODTHIRSTY AND BLACKHEARTED PIRATES EVER TO PROWL THE SEVEN SEAS!

AND AT THEIR HEAD, THE MOST UNHOLY MURDEROUS PIRATE OF THEM ALL, THE DREADED *DOGBEARD!*

I KNEW THEY WOULD FIND US BELOW SOON ENOUGH. AND THERE WERE NO CHANCE OF SURVIVAL IF I WENT ABOVE, SO I SWUNG OUT THE PORTHOLE, LEAVIN' THE COOK BEHIND.

I SCRAMBLED ALOFT INTO THE RIGGING, SURVEYING THE MELEE BELOW.

AHRRRR-DIDDLY-DAHRRR!

PUPPIES!! YIIEEEE!!

WITH THE FEARSOME COMMOTION SWIRLING BELOW, NOT A MAN THOUGHT TO TEND TO THE HELM. OUR PATHETIC OLD BUCKET WAS AT THE MERCY OF THE GALE-LIKE WINDS WHICH HAD BLOWN UP SUDDENLY.

AND AS LADY LUCK WOULD HAVE IT, THE WINDS WERE A-BLOW US REMORSELESSLY STRAIGHT INTO A HUGE *ICEBERG*...

...WHICH WAS FRONTED BY A POWERFUL AND VIOLENT *MAELSTROM!*

STILL THE PANDEMONIUM OF PIRATES AND THEIR PREY RAGED BELOW, OBLIVIOUS TO THE IMPENDING DISASTER!

WHEN FROM THE UNFATHOMABLE DEPTHS OF THIS ICY AND MALIGNANT SEA BROKE A HORROR THE MERE *SIGHT* OF WHICH WOULD FREEZE THE BLOOD OF THE *BRAVEST* MAN.

D JUST AS THE MAELSTROM PITCHED THE
TTLE-RAVAGED "INSIPID" INTO THE ICEBERG,
E *GIANT SQUID* CRESTED THE SEA ALMOST
VOURING THE SHIP. A MASSIVE TENTACLE
THERED AROUND ME *LEG*, SNAPPED OFF THE
ST TO WHICH I CLUNG, AND I WAS HURLED
FELY FREE OF THE FLAMING, SINKING HULK.

BUT SO FAR AS I KNOW, ME LEG IS STILL
WHIRLING AROUND IN THOSE EVIL WATERS,
PINNED TO THE MAST OF THE "INSIPID."

AND *THAT* BE THE
STORY OF HOW I GOT
ME *PEG LEG*. ENJOY
YOUR MEAL.

AAH-HAR-HARR,
HA-HA-HA-HA-HA-
HA-HA-HARRR!

HEY, THAT GUY
DOESN'T HAVE A
PEG LEG!

YES, AND THESE
SEAFOOD FINGERS *DON'T
HAVE* ANY SEAFOOD IN
THEM EITHER.

THE END.

SCRIPT
JAMIE ANGELL

PENCILS
PHIL ORTIZ

INKS
TIM BAVINGTON

LETTERS
JEANNINE BLACK

COLORS
NATHAN KANE

LANDLUBBER
MATT GROENING

SCRIPT
DOUG TUBER &
TIM MAILE

PENCILS &
ART SUPERVISION
STEPHANIE GLADDEN

INKS
TIM HARKINS &
TIM BAVINGTON

LETTERS
JEANNINE CROWELL
BLACK

COLORS
NATHAN
KANE

2 18 1 9 14 9 1 3
MATT
GROENING

MOMENTS LATER...

HOMER, YOU'RE A FINE FATHER, BUT SOMETIMES YOU'RE A COMPLETE *NINNY!* TALK TO LISA.

WHY DON'T *YOU* DO THAT, AND *I'LL* WAIL THE BEJABBERS OUT OF BART. THAT'S MORE MY AREA OF EXPERTISE.

YOU OWE LISA AN *APOLOGY AND A NEW SAXOPHONE.* NOW GET IN THERE, OR THERE'LL BE *NO DESSERT.*

F W O O S H!

IT'S JUST MUSIC, SWEETHEART.

"JUST" MUSIC? DO YOU *REALIZE* HOW MANY HIDING PLACES MY SOUL CAN FIND BEHIND THE EIGHT NOTES IN A SINGLE OCTAVE?

I GUESS I DON'T... *"BAD, BAD LEROY BROWN"* MADE ME *CRY* ONCE.

I'LL GET YOU A *NEW* SAXOPHONE, NO MATTER *HOW MUCH* IT COSTS.

THEY'RE UPWARDS OF *400 DOLLARS.*

OR I COULD GET YOU A *DIFFERENT* INSTRUMENT-- A *BETTER* INSTRUMENT! HOW 'BOUT A JEW'S HARP? OR A SLIDE-WHISTLE--YOU KNOW THAT'S MY FAVORITE. *MAYBE BOTH.*

THANK YOU, FATHER.

Lardo Chipz

Duff

:SIGH:

ZCHOMP, CHOMP!Z
MMMM...NASTURTIUM-Y...

DON'T OPEN THIS DOOR, OR LOTS OF OUR *CIVILIZATION WILL PERISH!* BYE, EVERYBODY!

SLAM!

EXPERIMENTAL HYPER-RADIATION LAB

ROOM C NEURO-PSYCHOLOGY LAB

GO FOR IT-- IT'S THE TAXPAYER'S MONEY.

HELLOOO, ANY SCIENTISTS HOME?... *YOO-HOO,* BRAINIACS? HOMER SIMPSON HERE--I'VE COME FOR YOUR EXPERIMENT. THE ONE THAT PAYS *500 SMACKEROONIES.*

AW, I SPILLED *INK* ALL OVER MYSELF. SO, YOU'RE HERE FOR THE *INTELLIGENCE EXPERIMENT*... HOW MANY JUSTICES ARE ON THE SUPREME COURT?

THE NEXT MORNING...

HERE'S YOUR MORNING PAPER, HOMER.

I THINK I'LL READ THE *NATIONAL SECTION* FIRST.

WHAT'S A PLACE IN THE NATION? WHAT'S HAPPENING IN, SAY, *MARGARITAVILLE*?

DENG ON THE WHITE HOUSE LAWN

BUT YOU NEVER READ *ANYTHING* EXCEPT *HAGAR THE HORRIBLE*. *THAT* USUALLY TAKES YOU MOST OF THE MORNING.

I WANT TO TELL YOU THIS GENTLY BECAUSE YOU'RE MY FAMILY AND I LOVE YOU... I'M INVOLVED IN A *STRANGE SCIENCE EXPERIMENT*. I TOOK A WEIRD PILL, AND I'M GOING TO CHANGE INTO A *TOTALLY* DIFFERENT PERSON YOU *WON'T RECOGNIZE*. PASS THE SYRUP, BART.

YOU DID THIS WITHOUT *TELLING* US? *WHY*?

TWO WORDS: "*CASH MONEY!*" BESIDES, I THOUGHT YOU'D *LIKE* A SMART HOMER. N I'LL BE ABLE TO UNDERSTAND T PHRASE, "SIX OF ONE, HALF-A DOZEN OF THE OTHER."

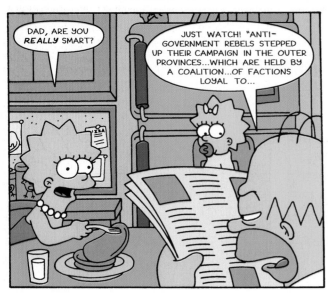

DAD, ARE YOU *REALLY* SMART?

JUST WATCH! "ANTI-GOVERNMENT REBELS STEPPED UP THEIR CAMPAIGN IN THE OUTER PROVINCES...WHICH ARE HELD BY A COALITION...OF FACTIONS LOYAL TO...

IT DIDN'T WORK! I'M STILL A *LOOBALL!* AW, WHAT'S THE *USE*?

SEE, HAGAR NEEDS A *HAIRCUT*, SO HE DOES IT HIMSELF WITH HIS *SWORD*. HE'S *EVERYMAN*, BUT HE'S A *VIKING!*

GUESS IT WAS TOO MUCH TO HOPE FOR.

I'M JUST TOO DUMB TO BE SMART. I FEEL SO *ATRABILIOUS.*

WHAT DID YOU SAY?

"ATRABILIOUS"... ADJECTIVE: DOWNHEARTED, DEJECTED...

...TO BE IN LOW SPIRITS. WOEFUL.

IT'S STARTING TO *WORK!*

DAD, YOU REALLY *ARE* SMART!

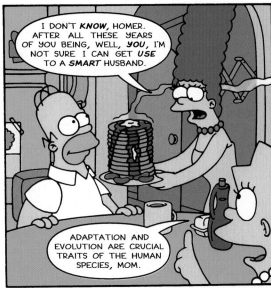

I DON'T *KNOW*, HOMER. AFTER ALL THESE YEARS OF YOU BEING, WELL, *YOU*, I'M NOT SURE I CAN GET *USE* TO A *SMART* HUSBAND.

ADAPTATION AND EVOLUTION ARE CRUCIAL TRAITS OF THE HUMAN SPECIES, MOM.

YEAH. AND IF YOU DON'T BELIEVE US, JUST ASK THE *MISSING LINK*... AND HERE HE *IS!* LOOK, LISA--I'M MAKING *EVOLUTION-SAUSAGE* JOKES!

HERE, BRAINMAN. I'VE ARRANGED ALL THE HOMEWORK BY DATE, STARTING WITH LAST FEBRUARY. AND DON'T FORGET, *WRITE LIKE A KID!*

HRRRM...

SKRITCH! SKRITCH!

THAT'S *BURKINA FASO,* FORMERLY *"UPPER VOLTA,"* IN AFRICA. MAJOR EXPORT, LIVESTOCK... "M-L-8, M-L-8." AS IN *"I'M LATE, I'M LATE FOR A VERY IMPORTANT DATE,"* FROM *"ALICE IN WONDERLAND."* IT WOULD BE APPROPRIATE ON A *WHITE VW RABBIT.*

ALBERT EINSTEIN
ALBERT SCHWEITZER
ALBERT BROOKS
PRINCE ALBERT
FAT ALBERT

ML-8

YOO SUNK MY BATTLESHIP, DRAT *YOOO!*

CARE FOR A LITTLE HOME VERSION OF *"TIC-TAC-DOUGH,"* MY BOVINE FRIEND?

MR. SIMPSON, *WELCOME* TO THE *WORLD OF SMARTNESS!*

GRRR-EAT TO BE HERE!

HYPERDYNAMIC NEWTONISM

Being and Nothingness and You

ADVANCED QUANTUM PHYSICS IN ARAMAIC

Stephen Hawkings Explains the Balk Rule

Stephen Hawkings Explains the Balk Rule, Vol. II

I, CLAUDIUS

AVE CLAUDIUS

THERE *IS* A ⟨AHEM⟩ CATCH. THE *PILL* YOU TOOK *WILL* MAKE YOUR CENTRAL NERVOUS SYSTEM FAIL AND IN 7 DAYS YOU'LL BE ⟨GAA⟩ *DEAD.*

WHAT?!

NEURO-PSYCHOLOGIST HUMOR. ACTUALLY, THE ENZYME LASTS 7 DAYS, THEN *SURGERY* CAN MAKE YOUR ⟨WEE HOO⟩ MENTAL PROWESS *PERMANENT.* THEN YOU'LL GET YOUR MONEY.

WHO NEEDS *MONEY* WHEN THERE'S *MONET?* I'M A *PUNSTER!*

HYPERDYNAMIC NEWTONISM

Being and Nothingness and You

ADVANCED QUANTUM PHYSICS IN ARAMAIC

FRENCH ⟨⟩RESSIONISM

AT AFTERNOON... LET'S SEE "...FROM *UP-TIGHTEN* OF BOLT *A* IN *FULLNESS OF BIKE*, SAY TO SELF '*YES!*' (DIAGRAM C), THEN *HAPPY SOUND OCCURS LEAVING NOTHING TO HOPE AT*." DARN *JAPANESE* INSTRUCTIONS!

STEP ASIDE, FLANDERS... COMPUTER TRANSLATIONS CAN'T INTUITIVELY GRASP VERNACULAR. BETTER JUST TO *READ THE JAPANESE.*

THREE MINUTES LATER...

ONLY 3 *MINUTES*, AND YOU MADE A *TEN-SPEED* OUT OF A *STING-RAY!* THINK YOU COULD GIVE ME A LEG-UP WITH MY SATELLITE DISH?

もんたッ たいよ*

* PIECE OF CAKE!

HOMER, YOU *ACED* MY HOMEWORK AND GOT EXTRA CREDIT FOR USING "*WICKIUP*" IN A SENTENCE. NOW THAT SCHOOLWORK WON'T MAKE INSANE DEMANDS ON MY TIME, WHAT SAY WE TOSS THE PIGSKIN AROUND?

I DON'T KNOW, SON-- THERE'S A NEW EXHIBIT AT THE PLANETARIUM--"*VENUS: COY MAIDEN OF THE NIGHT SKY, OR POISONOUS PREVIEW OF EARTH'S TOMORROW?*" WANNA GO?

OH, SURE. AND AFTER THAT, YOU CAN *STACK ROCKS* ON MY HEAD UNTIL I *DIE*.

I'D LIKE TO GO, DAD.

GREAT! STAND BACK, WORLD--*SMART PEOPLE COMING THROUGH!*

FEW DAYS LATER...

SPRINGFIELD CULTURAL CENTER

WOW, A *RODIN SCULPTURE EXHIBIT*, THE *SWAN LAKE BALLET*, AND A 32-PIECE ORCHESTRA PLAYING THE *1812 OVERTURE*, WITH *CANNON*. THERE'S MORE *ROOM* IN THERE THAN YOU'D *THINK*.

EXCELLENT SPATIAL DYNAMICS. THOUGH I *DID* FIND THE *LIPIZZANER STALLIONS* SOMEWHAT MIDDLEBROW. THERE'S NO NEED TO *PANDER*.

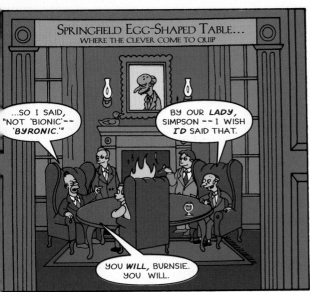

SPRINGFIELD EGG-SHAPED TABLE...
WHERE THE CLEVER COME TO QUIP

...SO I SAID, "NOT 'BIONIC'-- '*BYRONIC*.'"

BY OUR *LADY*, SIMPSON -- I WISH *I'D* SAID THAT.

YOU *WILL*, BURNSIE. YOU WILL.

HA HA!

BEDAD, HOMER, YOU WIELD WIT LIKE A *SURGEON'S SCALPEL*.

HO-HO HRUMPF!

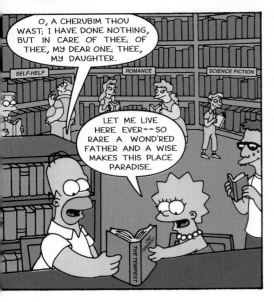

O, A CHERUBIM THOU WAST; I HAVE DONE NOTHING, BUT IN CARE OF THEE; OF THEE, MY DEAR ONE; THEE, MY DAUGHTER.

SELF-HELP

ROMANCE

SCIENCE FICTION

LET ME LIVE HERE EVER--SO RARE A WOND'RED FATHER AND A WISE MAKES THIS PLACE PARADISE.

MR. SIMPSON? THAT COPY OF "*LYING AROUND EATING AND BURPING FOR DUMMIES*" YOU ORDERED LAST WEEK IS HERE.

LYING AROUND EATING AND BURPING FOR DUMMIES

BEGONE, CHURL-- PRESUME *NOT* I AM THAT MAN I WAS. DON'T DRAG YOUR SORRY SELF AROUND ME *AGAIN*, OR I'LL SEE YOU BOUNCED *OUT* OF HERE!

EASY, DAD. YOU'RE NOT USED TO BEING *SMART*, YET. SOMETIMES IT TAKES *PATIENCE* TO DEAL WITH PEOPLE WHO AREN'T AS SMART AS YOU.

THAT EVENING...

HOW CAN SCRATCHY *STILL* BE *SWORD FIGHTING*? ITCHY CUT HIS HEAD OFF WITH *PRUNING SHEARS*.

SPURT!

GURGLE!

CLOSE CAPTIONED FOR THE HEARING IMPAIRED.

WRONG! THE FORCE OF GRAVITY IS *CONSTANT*. HE SHOULD DROP LIKE A *STONE*. I'M CHANGING THE CHANNEL.

CLICK!

AAAAH!

ANACHRONISM! DINOSAURS DIDN'T LIVE WITHIN A *MILLION* YEARS OF *AUSTRALOPITHECUS*. THIS IS DRIVING ME *MAD!*

"20 MILLION YEARS BEFORE TIME." COOOOL.

I NEED *AIR!*

DAD'S NO *FUN* ANYMORE. I DON'T EVEN LIKE *WATCHING TV* WITH HIM.

I'M *WORRIED*--I'M AFRAID I'M LOSING YOUR FATHER. I DON'T THINK I *WANT* HIM TO STAY SMART.

I WANT HIM TO STAY SMART! YOU'RE AFRAID OF *LOSING* HIM? WELL, I JUST *FOUND* HIM--AND HE'S *MINE*, DO YOU HEAR? *MINE, MINE, MINE!*

ARE YOU OKAY, DAD?

WHAT'S *HAPPENING*?! I THOUGHT I'D BE *HAPPY* BEING A GENIUS. BUT I SEE THINGS THAT *ANNOY* ME. AND I *YELLED AT YOUR MOTHER*... IT *SUCKS* BEING SMART.

SEE THAT STAR, DAD? THE ONE OFF BY ITSELF? THAT USED TO BE *ME*--A TINY LIGHT, *ALONE* IN A *HOSTILE UNIVERSE*.

NOW THERE'S *TWO OF US*. WE'RE LIKE THAT BINARY SYSTEM SHINING THERE NEAR THE FLANDERS' CHIMNEY.

YOUR SEVEN DAYS OF GENIUS EXPIRE TOMORROW-- YOU COULD GO BACK TO BEING...

I CAN'T *SAY* IT.

I CAN'T LET YOU BE A LONELY LITTLE STAR. GOING BACK TO BEING DUMB WOULD BE...*NOT SMART.*

THE NEXT DAY...

I DIDN'T KNOW COLLEGE HAD SO MUCH TO OFFER... BUT I DON'T SEE WHY WE HAD TO GET ALL DUDED UP JUST SO *DAD* COULD HAVE A *DUMBECTOMY*.

BECAUSE, YOUR FATHER IS ABOUT TO START A *NEW LIFE* WHERE HE'LL NEVER AGAIN BE THE SIMPLE HUSBAND AND FATHER WE KNOW AND LOVE.

GOOD LUCK WITH THAT, HOMER. DROP ME A POSTCARD FROM *SMARTSVILLE*-- I'LL BE WATCHING THE LUNG TRANSPLANT IN OPERATION THEATER C.

MOMENTS LATER, IN THE LAB...

WE'LL BE READY IN A MOMENT, MR. ¿AHUM¿ SIMPSON. IF YOU'LL JUST WAIT HERE...

THESE PEOPLE SURE HAVEN'T DELIVERED WHAT THEY *PROMISED*.

SUPER INTELLIGENCE FOUND ONLY IN SOMEONE WITH A CRANIUM THE SIZE OF A MEDICINE BALL?

REFRESHMENT I HAVEN'T SEEN HI¿ NOR HAIR OF A MAC¿ ROON SINCE I'VE BE¿ *COMING* HER¿

HMM, THE PILL MUST BE WEARING OFF. THERE'S THE OLD HOMER I KNOW AND LOVE.

OH... HAGAR THE HORRIBLE'S WENCH TELLS HIM HE SHOULD GO ON A *DIET* BECAUSE HIS *PANTS* WON'T FIT, SO HE CUTS THE WAISTBAND WITH HIS SWORD AND PUTS THEM ON... THAT'S NOT *FUNNY*, THAT'S *DUMB*.

TIME TO PREP YOU, MR. SIMPSON.

SEE YOU LATER, DAD?

YOU BET, SWEET- HEART. WE'LL GO TO THE MUSEUM AND CHECK OUT THAT NEW EXHIBIT ON THE BALANCE OF NATURE.

BYE, HOMER.

BYE, MARGE.

¿SIGH¿

BALANCE OF
NATURE EXHIBIT?

IT SHOWS HOW MAN AND NATURE INTERACT IN A *FRAGILE* EQUILIBRIUM. IF ANY ELEMENT TIPS THE BALANCE, THE WHOLE NATURAL ORDER COULD UNRAVEL LIKE A *BULGARIAN SPORTS JACKET*.

I HOPE OUR *FAMILY* DOESN'T UNRAVEL. I WONDER WHAT WILL HAPPEN NOW THAT YOUR FATHER DOESN'T PAY MUCH ATTENTION TO BART.

I THINK BART CAN BE RELIED ON TO TAKE CARE OF *HIMSELF*.

BANZAI!

HOUSTON, WE HAVE A PROBLEM!

S·P·R·O·I·N·G·I·N·G·ING!

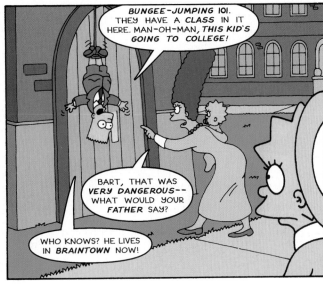

BUNGEE-JUMPING 101. THEY HAVE A *CLASS* IN IT HERE. MAN-OH-MAN, *THIS KID'S GOING TO COLLEGE!*

BART, THAT WAS *VERY DANGEROUS*-- WHAT WOULD YOUR *FATHER* SAY?

WHO KNOWS? HE LIVES IN *BRAINTOWN* NOW!

YOU'RE *MISERABLE* BEING SMART. INTELLIGENCE AND WISDOM ARE *DIFFERENT THINGS.* I WANT TO RESTORE THE NATURAL BALANCE OF OUR FAMILY--A WORLD WITH HOMER SIMPSON AS SMART AS SOCRATES IS LIKE A WORLD WITH *MOSQUITOES* THE *SIZE OF TWIN-ENGINE CESSNAS.*

BUT WHAT ABOUT *YOU,* SWEETHEART? YOU'LL BE ALL ALONE AGAIN.

I'LL *ALWAYS* HAVE PLASTER-OF-PARIS.

EXPERIMENT'S OFF! I WANT MY *FIVE HUNDRED BUCKS,* AND I WANT MY *BRAIN* BACK!

SHOOT. THAT MEANS I'LL HAVE TO GO BACK T *VIVISECTING SPACE ALIE* AND *MERMAIDS* TO FIND C WHAT MAKES 'EM *TICK.* ϶A HEM HOO϶

IF ANYBODY'S INTERESTED, THIS CLASSROOM DOWN THE HALL HAS A *BABY IN A JAR!*

LEMMESEE, LEMMESEE!

GOOD-BYE, FATHER...

AT EVENING...

THANKS FOR MY *NEW SAX*, DAD. IT'S EVEN *ETTER* THAN MY OLD ONE. WITH S BABY, I CAN *REALLY* POUR OUT E SENSE OF TORTURED ALIENATION I FEEL INSIDE. HOW CAN I EVER REPAY YOU?

EASY. BY PLAYING ON *STREET CORNERS* FOR *SPARE CHANGE*, AND PASSING IT ALONG *TO ME*.

HOMER, MAYBE YOU COULD TAKE *LISA* TO THE *CULTURAL CENTER* NEXT WEEKEND.

C'MON, MOM. THE OLD HOMER'S *BACK*--HE WOULDN'T KNOW *CULTURE* IF IT JUMPED UP AND BIT HIM IN THE BUTT.

YOU GOT *THAT* RIGHT. JUST LIKE IT TOOK ME *THREE DAYS* TO KNOW A *RACCOON* WHEN ONE BIT ME IN THE BUTT. IF I HADN'T *SAT* ON HIM, HE'D BE THERE TO THIS *DAY*!

HA, HAH, HEH! REMEMBER HOW IT WOULDN'T LET GO?

TEE-HEE-HEE! AND HOW YOU NEARLY GOT *RABIES*?!

AH, HAH, HA! THE JOKE *SURE* WAS ON *ME*!

THINGS ARE BACK TO *NORMAL*, AREN'T THEY, HOMEY?

HAAA, HA! YOU BET, MARGE. *RABIES*! FOURTEEN INCH *NEEDLES*, STUCK IN MY *STOMACH*! OH, THAT'S RICH! AHH, HAAAAAA-HA-HAAA!...

THE END.